HE CARRIED
OUR SORROWS

Copyright © 1983 Lion Publishing

Published by
Lion Publishing plc
Icknield Way, Tring, Herts, England
ISBN 0 85648 454 7 (casebound edition)
ISBN 0 7459 1072 6 (paperback edition)
Albatross Books Pty Ltd
PO Box 320, Sutherland, NSW 2232, Australia
ISBN 0 86760 311 9 (casebound edition)
ISBN 0 86760 694 0 (paperback edition)

Compiled by Ruth Connell

First edition 1983
Reprinted 1986
First paperback edition 1986

Isaiah 53 quoted from The Holy Bible, New
International Version: *copyright © New York
International Bible Society, 1978*

Other Bible quotations from:
Revised Standard Version, *copyright 1946 and
1952, second edition 1971, Division of Christian
Education, National Council of the Churches of
Christ in the USA*

British Library Cataloguing in Publication Data
[Bible. O.T. Isaiah LIII. *English. New
International. 1985*]
He carried our sorrows.—(Famous Bible passages)
I. He carried our sorrows II. Connell, Ruth
III. Series
224'.1052   BS1520.A3
ISBN 0 85648 454 7

Printed and bound in Great Britain by
Purnell and Sons (Book Production) Ltd,
Paulton, Bristol

Famous Bible Passages

HE CARRIED
OUR SORROWS

Isaiah 53

A LION BOOK

Tring · Belleville · Sydney

Who has believed our message
and to whom has the arm of the Lord been
revealed?
He grew up before him like a tender shoot,
and like a root out of dry ground.
He had no beauty or majesty to attract us to him,
nothing in his appearance that we should desire
him.
He was despised and rejected by men,
a man of sorrows, and familiar with suffering.
Like one from whom men hide their faces
he was despised, and we esteemed him not.
Surely he took up our infirmities
and carried our sorrows,
yet we considered him stricken by God,
smitten by him, and afflicted.
But he was pierced for our transgressions,
he was crushed for our iniquities;
the punishment that brought us peace was upon
him,
and by his wounds we are healed.
We all, like sheep, have gone astray,
each of us has turned to his own way;
and the Lord has laid on him the iniquity of us all.
He was oppressed and afflicted,
yet he did not open his mouth;
he was led like a lamb to the slaughter,

and as a sheep before her shearers is silent,
so he did not open his mouth.
By oppression and judgment,
he was taken away.
And who can speak of his descendants?
For he was cut off from the land of the living;
for the transgression of my people he was stricken.
He was assigned a grave with the wicked,
and with the rich in his death,
though he had done no violence,
nor was any deceit in his mouth.
Yet it was the Lord's will to crush him and cause
him to suffer,
and though the Lord makes his life a guilt offering,
he will see his offspring and prolong his days,
and the will of the Lord will prosper in his hand.
After the suffering of his soul,
he will see the light of life and be satisfied;
by his knowledge my righteous servant will justify many,
and he will bear their iniquities.
Therefore I will give him a portion among the great,
and he will divide the spoils with the strong,
because he poured out his life unto death,
and was numbered with the transgressors.
For he bore the sin of many,
and made intercession for the transgressors.

Isaiah 53

In all ages these words concerning the one called the 'servant of the Lord' have been beloved by Christians for the portrait they paint of our crucified master. We find these same words echoing in the New Testament, not only because they are beautiful words to describe Christ and his sacrifice on behalf of sinful humanity, but also because they constitute a call to the Christian to do likewise.

John Howard Yoder

Who has believed our message and to whom has the arm of the Lord been revealed?

The god of this age has blinded the minds of unbelievers, so that they cannot see the light of the gospel of the glory of Christ, who is the image of God.

2 Corinthians 4:4

Though Jesus had done so many signs before them, yet they did not believe him; it was that the word spoken by the prophet Isaiah might be fulfilled:
'Lord, who has believed our report,
and to whom has the arm of the Lord been revealed?'

John 12: 37–38

Jesus said: 'I praise you, Father, Lord of heaven and earth, because you have hidden these things from the wise and learned, and revealed them to little children. Yes, Father, for this was your good pleasure.'

Matthew 11: 25–26

It does not detract from the gospel of Christ if few be the disciples to receive it. Nor does the fewness of believers lessen its authority or obscure its infinite glory. On the contrary, the very sublimity of its mystery is a reason why it hardly meets with faith in the world. For it is folly, because it transcends all human senses.

John Calvin

Jesus said, 'He who has ears to hear, let him hear.'

Mark 4:9

He grew up before him like a tender shoot,
and like a root out of dry ground.

There shall come forth a shoot from the stump of Jesse,
and a branch shall grow out of his roots.
And the Spirit of the Lord shall rest upon him,
the spirit of wisdom and understanding,
the spirit of counsel and might,
the spirit of knowledge and the fear of the Lord.
And his delight shall be in the fear of the Lord.
Isaiah 11: 1–3

Our Saviour is a root that derives nothing from the soil in which it grows but puts everything into the soil. Christ does not live because of his surroundings, but he makes those to live who are around him.
Charles Haddon Spurgeon

Jesus said, 'I tell you the truth, the Son can do nothing by himself; he can do only what he sees his Father doing, because whatever the Father does the Son also does.'
John 5:19

Jesus himself did not derive his life and strength from outward circumstances. Nor must we ... The secret source of our life is God alone.
Watchman Nee

*He had no beauty or majesty
to attract us to him,
nothing in his appearance
that we should desire him.*

---

*The Lord sees not as man sees; man looks on the outward
appearance, but the Lord looks on the heart.*

1 Samuel 16:7

---

*Coming to his home town, Jesus began teaching the people in
their synagogue, and they were amazed. 'Where did this man
get this wisdom and these miraculous powers?' they asked.
'Isn't this the carpenter's son? Isn't his mother's name Mary,
and aren't his brothers James, Joseph, Simon and Judas?
Aren't all his sisters with us? Where then did this man get
all these things?' And they took offence at him.*

Matthew 13: 54–57

---

*A scribe came up and said to him, 'Teacher, I will follow you
wherever you go.' And Jesus said to him, 'Foxes have holes,
and birds of the air have nests; but the Son of man has
nowhere to lay his head.'*

Matthew 8:19–20

You know the grace of our Lord Jesus Christ, that though he was rich, yet for your sake he became poor, so that by his poverty you might become rich.

2 Corinthians 8 : 9

A man is what he appears in God's eyes, and not the slightest bit more.

Francis of Assisi

He was despised and rejected by men . . .
Like one from whom men hide their faces
he was despised, and we esteemed him not.

The true light that gives light to every man was coming into
the world. He was in the world, and though the world was
made through him, the world did not recognise him. He came
to that which was his own, but his own did not receive him
. . . Light has come into the world, but men loved darkness
instead of light because their deeds were evil.

John 1:9–11; 3:19

If you resort with devotion to the wounds and precious scars of
Jesus, you will find great comfort in trouble. You will not
mind so much if men despise you, and you will find it easy to
bear when they speak against you. Christ too was despised by
men in this world, and in his greatest need was abandoned by
friends and followers and left to face humiliation. Christ was
prepared to suffer and to be despised. Dare you raise any
complaint? Christ had enemies and detractors. Do you expect
to find everyone a friend and benefactor? How can you be
rewarded for endurance if you have never met anything that
has to be endured? If you are not prepared to suffer opposition,
how can you be a friend of Christ? You must endure with
Christ and for the sake of Christ, if you wish to reign with
Christ.

Thomas à Kempis.

The whole of our Lord's life is an offence to the wisdom of this world; his lowly birth, his upbringing, his education, his followers, his self-identification with human sin, which the prophet pictures in its symbols of pain and sickness.
H. L. Ellison

Jesus did not promise his own that they would not suffer, he promised a serenity beyond human reach because it has its source in him.
Léon Joseph

Blessed are you when men revile you and persecute you and utter all kinds of evil against you falsely on my account.
Matthew 5:11

15

A man of sorrows, and familiar with suffering

Sin was laid upon him, and he was himself numbered with the transgressors, and therefore he was called to bear the terrible blows of divine justice, and suffered unknown, immeasurable agonies.

Charles Haddon Spurgeon

It was the third hour, when they crucified him . . . And when the sixth hour had come, there was darkness over the whole land until the ninth hour. And at the ninth hour Jesus cried with a loud voice 'Eloi, Eloi, lama sabachthani?' which means 'My God, my God, why hast thou forsaken me?'

Mark 15:25, 33–34

Suffering means being cut off from God. Therefore those who live in communion with him cannot really suffer. This Old Testament doctrine was expressly reaffirmed by Jesus. That is why he takes upon himself the suffering of the whole world, and in doing so proves victorious over it. He bears the whole burden of man's separation from God, and in the very act of drinking the cup he causes it to pass over him. He sets out to overcome the suffering of the world, and so he must drink it to the dregs. Hence while it is still true that suffering means being cut off from God, yet within the fellowship of Christ's suffering, suffering is overcome by suffering, and becomes the way to communion with God.

Dietrich Bonhoeffer

He had to be made like his brothers in every way, in order that he might make atonement for the sins of the people. Because he himself suffered when he was tempted, he is able to help those who are being tempted.

Hebrews 2:17–18

*S*urely he took up our infirmities and carried our sorrows

Jesus Christ was laden with all our sins and iniquities; not at all because he was guilty of them, but because he was willing for them all to be imputed to himself, and to render account for them and make the payment.

John Calvin

Now I saw in my Dream, that the high way up which Christian was to go, was fenced on either side with a Wall, and that Wall is called Salvation. Up this way therefore did burdened Christian run, but not without great difficulty, because of the load on his back.

He ran thus till he came at a place somewhat ascending; and upon that place stood a Cross, and a little below in the bottom, a Sepulchre. So I saw in my Dream, that just as Christian came up with the Cross, his burden loosed from off his shoulders, and fell from off his back; and began to tumble, and so continued to do, till it came to the mouth of the Sepulchre, where it fell in, and I saw it no more.

Then was Christian glad and lightsom, and said with a merry heart, he hath given me rest, by his sorrow; and life, by his death . . . Then Christian gave three leaps for joy, and went out singing.

John Bunyan, from 'The Pilgrim's Progress'

He who takes his neighbour's burden upon himself . . . he, I say, is an imitator of God!

The Epistle to Diognetus

*Y*et we considered him stricken by God,
smitten by him, and afflicted.

---

*Those who passed by (the cross) derided Jesus, wagging their
heads and saying, 'You who would destroy the temple and
build it in three days, save yourself! If you are the Son of
God, come down from the cross.' So also the chief priests with
the scribes and elders, mocked him, saying, 'He saved others;
he cannot save himself. He is the King of Israel; let him come
down now from the cross, and we will believe in him. He trusts
in God; let God deliver him now, if he desires him; for he
said, 'I am the Son of God.' And the robbers who were
crucified with him also reviled him in the same way.*

Matthew 27:39–44

---

*Self-righteously, like Job's friends, we thought that such
sufferings could be interpreted only as divine retribution for vile
personal sins; surely the Servant was smitten by God. How
could we be so stupid? . . . The torments the Servant endured
were ours. We were the guilty ones, and his sufferings were the
retribution for our vile personal sins. It was for our sake that
he submitted himself to undeserved punishment, that we might
be healed.*

Henri Blocher

But he was pierced for our transgressions, he was crushed for our iniquities

Very rarely will anyone die for a righteous man, though for a good man someone might possibly dare to die. But God demonstrates his own love for us in this: While we were still sinners, Christ died for us.

Romans 5 : 7–8

God, in a mysterious way, caused him, our sinless Redeemer, to become identified with human sin, our sin, in order that we, who are anything but sinless, might become identified with righteousness, not our own but God-given.

H.E. Guillebaud

Jesus said, 'I am the good shepherd; I know my own and my own know me, as the Father knows me and I know the Father; and I lay down my life for the sheep . . . For this reason the Father loves me, because I lay down my life, that I may take it again. No one takes it from me, but I lay it down of my own accord.'

John 10 : 14–15, 17–18

No man besides him ever gave to God, by dying, what he was not necessarily going to lose at some time, or paid what he did not owe. But this man freely offered to the Father what he would never have lost by any necessity, and paid for sinners what he did not owe for himself.

Anselm

The punishment that brought us peace was upon him, and by his wounds we are healed.

He was stricken because he received into his soul the penalty of human guilt. He stood before the universe charged with the sins of the race, and their consequence. He tasted death for every man. He was so identified with sin, its shame, suffering, and penalty that he deemed himself forsaken by God. In that one act of the cross he put away sin, exhausted the penalty, wiped out the guilt, and laid the foundation of a redemption which includes the whole family of man.

F.B. Meyer

He himself bore our sins in his body on the tree, that we might die to sin and live to righteousness. By his wounds you have been healed. For you were straying like sheep, but have now returned to the Shepherd and Guardian of your souls.

1 Peter 2:24–25

Since we are justified by faith, we have peace with God through our Lord Jesus Christ. Through him we have obtained access to this grace in which we stand, and we rejoice in our hope of sharing the glory of God.

Romans 5:1–2

His chastisement is the remedy that brings peace to our conscience . . . He was chastised for the sake of our peace.

Martin Luther

God cannot give us a happiness and peace apart from himself, because it is not there. There is no such thing.

C.S. Lewis

Peace
Is what happens
When Heaven and Earth
Overlap.
Andrew Knowles

We all, like sheep, have gone astray,
each of us has turned to his own way;
and the Lord has laid on him
the iniquity of us all.

St Paul's definition of sin is 'falling short of the glory of
God.' It is quite impossible to estimate the amount of harm
done by our habitual limitation of the use of the word 'sin' to
deliberate wrong-doing. Everything about us is sin if it is not
what God wants it to be.
William Temple

We did not seek to follow the way God had laid down for us
but sought rather our own way, and in thus doing we glorified
the creature rather than the creator. We were selfish, and the
result of our selfish action was that we became lost.
Edward J. Young

The Son of man came to seek and to save the lost.
Luke 19:10

Each one of us ought to look to himself and his faults if he
would acquire a love for the death and passion of our Lord
Jesus Christ.
John Calvin

He was oppressed and afflicted,
yet he did not open his mouth;
he was led like a lamb to the slaughter,
and as a sheep before her shearers is silent,
so he did not open his mouth.

John the Baptist 'saw Jesus coming towards him, and said,
"Behold the Lamb of God, who takes away the sin of the
world".'

John 1:29

After his arrest Jesus was brought before Pilate. 'When he
was accused by the chief priests and elders, he made no answer.
Then Pilate said to him, "Do you not hear how many things
they testify against you?" But he gave him no answer, not
even to a single charge; so that the governor wondered greatly.'

Matthew 27: 12–14

The oceans of history are made turbulent by the ever-rising
tides of revenge. Man has never risen above the injunction of
the 'lex talionis': 'Life for life, eye for eye, tooth for tooth,
hand for hand, foot for foot.' In spite of the fact that the law
of revenge solves no social problems, men continue to follow its
disastrous leading. Jesus eloquently affirmed from the cross a
higher law. He knew that the old eye-for-an-eye philosophy
would leave everyone blind. He did not seek to overcome evil
with evil. He overcame evil with good. Although crucified by
hate, he responded with aggressive love.

Martin Luther King Jnr

---

*The only way to overcome evil is to let it run itself to a
standstill because it does not find the resistance it is looking for.
Resistance merely creates further evil and adds fuel to the
flames. But when evil meets no opposition and encounters no
obstacle but only patient endurance, its sting is drawn, and at
last it meets an opponent which is more than its match.*

Dietrich Bonhoeffer

*Christ suffered for you, leaving you an example, that you
should follow in his steps. 'He committed no sin, and no deceit
was found in his mouth.' When they hurled their insults at
him, he did not retaliate; when he suffered, he made no
threats. Instead, he entrusted himself to him who judges justly.*

1 Peter 2:21–23

*By oppression and judgment,
he was taken away.
And who can speak of his descendants?
For he was cut off from the land of the living;
for the transgression of my people he was stricken.*

---

*The people of Jerusalem and their rulers did not recognise
Jesus, yet in condemning him they fulfilled the words of the
prophets that are read every Sabbath. Though they found no
proper ground for a death sentence, they asked Pilate to have
him executed.*

Acts 13:27–28

---

*God so loved the world that he gave his only Son, that
whoever believes in him should not perish but have eternal life.
For God sent the Son into the world, not to condemn the
world, but that the world might be saved through him.*

John 3:16–17

*He was assigned a grave with the wicked,
and with the rich in his death,
though he had done no violence,
nor was any deceit in his mouth.*

---

*As evening approached, there came a rich man from
Arimathea, named Joseph, who had himself become a disciple
of Jesus. Going to Pilate, he asked for Jesus' body, and Pilate
ordered that it be given to him. Joseph took the body, wrapped
it in a clean linen cloth, and placed it in his own new tomb
that he had cut out of the rock. He rolled a big stone in front
of the entrance to the tomb and went away.*

Matthew 27:57–60

---

*Though he died with the wicked, and according to the
common course of dealing with criminals should have been
buried with them in the place where he was crucified, yet God
here foretold, and Providence so ordered it, that he should
make his grave with the innocent, with the rich, as a mark of
distinction put between him and those that really deserved to
die, even in his sufferings.*

Matthew Henry

Yet it was the Lord's will to crush him and cause him to suffer

God was pleased to have all his fulness dwell in him, and through him to reconcile to himself all things, whether things on earth or things in heaven, by making peace through his blood, shed on the cross.

Colossians 1:19–20

None but God had power to lay our sins upon Christ, both because sin was committed against him and to him the satisfaction was to be made, and because Christ, on whom the iniquity was to be laid, was his own Son, the Son of his love, and his holy child Jesus, who himself knew no sin.

Matthew Henry

Paul, writing to the church at Ephesus, says:
'Although I am less than the least of all God's people, this grace was given to me: to preach to the Gentiles the unsearchable riches in Christ, and to make plain to everyone the administration of this mystery, which for ages past was kept hidden in God, who created all things. His intent was that now, through the church, the manifold wisdom of God should be made known to the rulers and authorities in the heavenly realms, according to his eternal purpose which he accomplished in Christ Jesus our Lord.'

Ephesians 3:8–11

*And though the Lord makes his life
a guilt offering,
he will see his offspring and prolong his days,
and the will of the Lord will prosper in his
hand.*

---

*Jesus said, 'Truly, truly, I say to you, unless a grain of wheat
falls into the earth and dies, it remains alone; but if it dies, it
bears much fruit.'*

John 12:24

---

*Although he was a Son, he learned obedience through what he
suffered; and being made perfect he became the source of eternal
salvation to all who obey him.*

Hebrews 5:8—9

---

*'Fear not, I am the first and the last, and the living one; I
died, and behold I am alive for evermore, and I have the keys
of Death and Hades.'*

Revelation 1:17—18

After the suffering of his soul,
he will see the light of life and be satisfied;
by his knowledge my righteous servant will
justify many, and he will bear their iniquities.

We see Jesus, who was made a little lower than the angels,
now crowned with glory and honour because he suffered death,
so that by the grace of God he might taste death for everyone.
Hebrews 2:9

Christ died for sins once for all, the righteous for the
unrighteous, to bring you to God. He was put to death in the
body but made alive by the Spirit.
1 Peter 3:18

God has saved us.
He has brought us out of slavery –
He has made the most expensive purchase in history.
And the price?
The life of his Son!

But there's no invoice.
It's free!

If God has given so generously to us
shouldn't we give generously to him?
Not because we have to,
but because we want to?

Andrew Knowles

Righteousness is the knowledge of Christ, who bears our iniquities. Whoever will, therefore, know and believe in Christ as bearing his sins will be righteous . . . There is no other plan or method of obtaining liberty than the knowledge of Christ.

Martin Luther

Jesus said:
'And I, when I am lifted up from the earth, will draw all men to myself.'

John 12:32

*Therefore I will give him a portion
among the great,
and he will divide the spoils with the strong,
because he poured out his life unto death,
and was numbered with the transgressors.*

*He who did not spare his own Son, but gave him up for us all
— how will he not also, along with him, graciously give us all
things?*

Romans 8:32

*Christ Jesus, 'being in very nature God,
did not consider equality with God
something to be grasped,
but made himself nothing,
taking the very nature of a servant,
being made in human likeness.
And being found in appearance as a man,
he humbled himself
and became obedient to death —
even death on a cross!
Therefore God exalted him to the highest place
and gave him the name that is above every name,
that at the name of Jesus every knee should bow,
in heaven and on earth and under the earth,
and every tongue confess that Jesus Christ is Lord,
to the glory of God the Father.'*

Philippians 2:6—11

Let us fix our eyes on Jesus, the author and perfector of our faith, who for the joy set before him endured the cross, scorning its shame, and sat down at the right hand of the throne of God.

Hebrews 12:2

Jesus the Son of man, . . . though lifted up to die, is by that very act lifted up to reign.

Watchman Nee

For he bore the sin of many,
and made intercession for the transgressors.

Jesus is able to save completely those who come to God through him, because he always lives to intercede for them.
Hebrews 7:25

He ascended to show the way to men, and to lead man with him.
He ascended to pray the Father for mankind.
John Wycliffe

Prayer

Thanks be to thee, my Lord Jesus Christ,
For all the benefits which thou hast given me,
For all the pains and insults which thou hast borne for me.
O most merciful Redeemer, Friend and Brother,
May I know thee more clearly,
Love thee more dearly,
And follow thee more nearly.

Richard of Chichester